It's Becoming A Lot More Difficult to Feel Unchanged

by
Adam Edelman

UnCollected Press

It's Becoming A Lot More Difficult to Feel Unchanged
Copyright © 2021 by Adam Edelman

All rights reserved. This book in full form may not be used or reproduced by electronic or mechanical means without permission in writing from the author and UnCollected Press.

Cover Art:
#3
Adam Edelman
12"x17" construction paper, magazines, glue

Back Cover Portrait:

Amrita Mishra

Book Design by:

UnCollected Press
8320 Main Street, 2nd Floor
Ellicott City, MD 21043

For more books by UnCollected Press:
www.therawartreview.com

First Edition 2021
ISBN: 978-1-7378731-3-6

Table of Contents

I Woke Up in a Field 1
Familiar Face 2
Paper Clips of Various Sizes 3
National Geographic 4
Carrying Half-Rotten Fruit Over the Platforms of the Floating World 5
The Vampire 6
Walking Home from the Hospital 7
This Poem Is No Longer in Use 8
The Franssen Effect 9
The Language of Flowers Is in Much Disrepair 10
In Pursuit of the Firebird 11
It's Becoming a Lot More Difficult to Feel Unchanged 12
To Be Written on the Back of a Ukiyo-e Postcard 13
Black Tea and Trakl 14
The Case of the Arm 15
Portrait of Tranströmer as a Fisherman 16
Dangerous Museum 17

for Ami & Kokoy

I Woke Up in a Field

One summer, in order to find out more
about my own fragility, I baled hay
inside a circle of river stones.
It was as if I was living and working
with another person, perhaps multiple.
This was in Montana. Every once in a while
a semi would pass on the highway
hidden by hills and I would look up
from my labor as if hearing the faint
but audible voice of a friend
I hadn't heard from in years.
Another routine involved
grilling meats, a little confession,
mediating between crickets
and toads. It thundered sporadically.
At some point I began to merely drift
over the contours of daily existence.
Then the barn caught fire.
The moon haloed the empty shell
a cricket left behind. Things
got darker from there, until all that was visible
was a little boy leading his baby goat
over the white hot coals.

Familiar Face

What held you to the loose wisps of night?
Even the yellow seat in view of the pier
has seen you as a figure with strange
capabilities, a silver cage of woods wolves
make tracks through, one drop of red paint
on a lily pad. For the first time ever, your shade
of a way we can imagine color looking
has an opportunity to interface with our devices
on a plain level. There were people selling things
in the streets. There was a time, and then it was gone.

Houses where we ate and heard music.
A tremor we each felt differently
came out of the fabrics and counters.
We had dreams of familiar towns
contrived from the past and future,
straw uprooted from the earth, labels
on packages, hands passing them onto
and off of conveyor belts and loading trucks.
I suppose it happened gradually.
We were looking for a place to cross the road
without getting our feet wet. We were noticing
in your shadow the light from the causeway

falling at such an angle so as not to seem like disguise,
and thereby transposing the anticipation of knowing
there is form and surface, but the real act takes place
on the cusp of periphery. It was a bright enough future,
not to mention all that was at stake, and all that wasn't
a meaningful contribution to the way we lived our lives
simmered beneath the aftermath of those aspects
of our circumstances for which we cannot account.

Nothing had changed after all. The chair fell asleep
and dreamed of being a chair. Remember when your
sadness merged with something outside you?
How did that feel?

Paper Clips of Various Sizes

Finally I can say I've seen all the local vegetables stuffed into bushels
and buckets, sampled the painful salsas and relish spreads, watched
a thin steam rise from the hot tamale stand in the slanting
Saturday rain. Finally I realize everything
crawling over the patches of clover is headed in the direction
of Antioch, California. Finally California is a magnet the shape of
      California
fixing a picture of my young parents on their honeymoon
through the Rockies to the freezer door. In a few weeks I will learn
what a kinglet looks like and I will spread coconut ice cream
over cut strawberries with Liszt's *Saint Francis of Assisi*
Preaching to the Birds running through my mind.
Even though I'm twenty-six and unfamiliar with the actual taste
of chai, I tell lies all the time, even to the faces of those
I am fully convinced I love. I think when I speak to you
about the old pane-less window frame
just hanging there wrapped with a green string of Christmas lights
I reclaim the nostalgia for your stuffy office of incognizable
pamphlets, paper clips of various sizes, your sliver
of white sunlight. I could be home in an hour and climb the greasy
      steps
to the upper floor with my right arm wrapped around the girl
you haven't met who, like me, like the bits of yellow leaf flipping over
and over down a flooding Upper Boggy Creek, can't remember
any of the smells from the time before mid-August, though
here in the dim bathroom in the back of the Elephant Room washing
my hands with coconut soap I sure am trying.

National Geographic

First I approximate the stampede patterns of gazelles
with a piece of sidewalk chalk, then the smell of myrtle.

I wear a crown of smokestacks just to be provocative.
The slats are crowded with statues and crumbs.

Usually I find some charred wood to sniff when I go
sleepwalking. I make peas and argue with a wall.

Something gets stuck like that. Once on a round planet
I saw a giant owl plastered all over a billboard.

On the way over here I took the definitive snapshot
of a stork.

Carrying Half-Rotten Fruit Over the Platforms of the Floating World

The look on the footbridge which the moon
unspells somehow includes or exposes.
Snowflakes dissolve on the ankle of the fire ant.
When they hear iron bells in a parking lot
sometimes thoughts don't make much noise
like a broken chimney or attic window
in the eyes of a stranger who is you as a child
forgetting your Mickey Mouse wristwatch
near a clogged grate on Catalina Island.
Later that evening we had purple beef tips.
The nail on the face of the room
always reminds me. The nail
tastes like the odor of sun-cloaked grain
lurking among tufts and briars.
After the winds erase roaming shadows
inside the eye of a coyote
and whirr dead air through an iron pipe
at the bottom of the well, I can tell you
the differences. A frozen tundra and the ear
of a streetlamp exchange envelopes
sealed forever, made of pure light.

The Vampire

I keep bumping into pockets of cooler air
and radiance as I dig through the mulch
to look for the teeth. The font of ontology
denies the soul to save the soul, and the body

has the weight of the voice I peel
off the smell of the rake-combed
lawn. My house should be done
burning by now. Like a lizard on a stone

I watch spiders carry their broken
talismans and silken towels. After
the sun goes down, after the weeded
lot is full of water and rotting
leaves, after the ant hills are ruined

I will remove the wooden gate
and place my hands on each new vegetable.

Walking Home from the Hospital

I'm tweaking the sticky knobs and breathing
on both mountains. The first few glowworms don't even
exist yet. I sweep some ash from a black pinecone
to prove this is what it feels like
to have one note in my breast pocket, to find
some shade and stand there an hour, not knowing
what my fingers do. That's when I have to kiss the buttons
on my long sleeve or bend my hand like a sunflower to open up
a bag of pears. I turn to a bird feeder. I pick up a vulture
feather and stick it to my forehead while my tongue goes numb.

This Poem Is No Longer in Use
After Larry Levis

If we chew the two colors
of the bad dream,
whole systems for a while
will live again.

In the distance of we are not
ourselves, to descend
to the ground of those who are paid
to touch the dead, we

followed. Through the palace
of tiny flowers, sweeping
wasn't working. Cattle
watched snow collect on the blind eye

of history. It is the cries
of what grows younger
with a new bouquet of dark
windows.

The Franssen Effect

This must be the part
where my hands are replaced
by hummingbirds.
Where little neon flags
designate where chemicals
to our sun-scorched yards
have been applied.
O there are cars here too,
and offices, hotels,
entire financial districts
marinating in what often feels
like a thick solution.
In one of the yards,
one of the hummingbirds
really drinks a flower.
It tends to come in fits
and bursts. Whether
for a couple of nights
or an hour, when the light
in those trees
seems small and I am led
a step further into that dark,
the stars lean in
to better hear the flags ripple
over all this noise.

The Language of Flowers is in Much Disrepair

Wildflowers are everywhere. You can go out
and find one if you look. What makes them wild?
It has been said they have a world of their own.
What makes them flowers? I like to imagine the petals
of a wildflower as slices of pizza, or frames
in a circular comic strip. Dumpsters have been spotted
in the vicinity of wildflowers, each a unique expression
of the desire to pass beyond suffering. Each wildflower
ingratiates a fluorescent zone. If you have a question
about wildflowers, the answer is yes. They control the weather,
and have been known to invade remote hamlets
under cover of darkness. Any good businessman will tell you
that the key to success is wildflowers. Neutrinos are a kind
of wildflower, if you think about it. Think of wildflowers
as a metaphor for good advice from a highly intelligent
and sensitive friend. Every human being who's ever lived
or died understands wildflowers. You can display them
in your home or dry them and hide them away if you choose.
If you melt down a box of warm colored crayons, distill
the pigment into a single drop and swallow it, you'll sneeze
wildflowers. Pick any wildflower. It can be transmuted
into medicine or spice. A pill bug once slept in a wildflower
for three and a half days. You literally can't do anything
without somehow involving at least one wildflower.
Tonight, when you're in your bed thinking of what
you'd like to dream about, just this once, consider
wildflowers; they were your face before you were born.

In Pursuit of the Firebird

Still, the heavens concoct influential themes
and variations—it's best not to fuck with them.

The train ride home from the airport
has its own particular feel, weighty

in a way I tend to enjoy less than the idea
of the totally singular iteration of return, god

as five ballerinas waiting in the wings
for their cue. Nothing's more militant

than treasure falling from all of the high-rises,
the marsh wielding me like a diamond, but most skies

find me recognizable if I'm a mile or less away
and standing in the right light. Pure joy

is in what's about to transpire there:
the inside of a tangelo before you unpeel it

resembles the lengthy trails of ducks and cranes
intermingling below Aurora Ave.

as loss drifts, leans on the element of flight.

It's Becoming a Lot More Difficult to Feel Unchanged

in Elgin when light's misting against the windshield
cracked last week by impact with a suddenly appearing
grackle off I-35, right after we left the backyard gathering
where several different people asked if you knew them
from earlier. When and where, neither of us could say
for sure, but it couldn't have been before that time we biked
to what we then called the nature trail, some Thanksgiving
or Easter in the early 2000s. Around then I was convinced
if I left the house key on the threshold of the breezeway
a clover would appear overnight. You'd taken up painting
the day your floral watch was delivered, and we organized
our lives into smaller and smaller units. It's true
I buried a robot-shaped tin under a maple at the city pool.
Pillowy steam rising between the roofs of two-stories
contributed to something, though we never found out what.
Perhaps a mood, but whose, who's to say? The problem
was similar to getting a feeling for one's room when no
one's in it, catching one's breath while the imagined
connection with that place with no walls, floor
or ceiling, ground or sky assembled piece by piece
in advance of us. For example, I arrived at the chrome
fountain in front of the diner across from the fiber optics
research park just as a commuter jet pierced the day
moon. A leak sprung up after breakfast that Thursday,
it didn't linger very long. I woke this morning without
a trace. Today in Elgin the culvert was flooded by runoff
from the township upstream, my neighbors have all
left for work. There's an image of a jaguar on the cover
of the road atlas someone left in the lobby; I appreciate
the palette they chose for the county population distribution
page, which teaches me how subtler hues can drift
through one another. Maybe at some point down the line
all this speculation, these initial glimmers that accommodate
our waking will be put to good use, but you never know.

To Be Written on the Back of a Ukiyo-e Postcard

Next time you drive past the scorched brick smokestacks
at Clinton and over the swimming pool blue cable bridge
into Morrison, Illinois, know that I'll be waiting for you
under waterlogged pines that leave a taste of day and night
to haunt the retina's fingerprint. Consider the picture by Hokusai,
the waterfall as unwavering as Li Po's staff, the roar
as deafening as unavailable. It absorbs enough of the attention
to make you forget the smoothed branch of violet lightning
he calls *The Kirifuri Falls in Mount Kurokami, Shimotsuke*
from his *Tour of the Falls in Various Provinces*. Their differences
unmediate. Treacherous narrow ledges
up and through cliff sides and the animal in one that leads
one's head beyond the visible as much as the blinking bulb
in the woodshed not contributing anything to the starless
expanse announces the dandelion as part of the background
—a distraction from all the mistakes. The edgeless wash
welling up in us touches a fissure behind what is seen:
a memento to the feelings of someone who lived once.
Changing one's face to better fit the mood of a gathering,
taking a deep breath before saying something personal,
one may describe these activities in great detail
so as to subvert the distance at which their correlation
comes into focus, everything in its place and accounted for.
The last thing the viewer will remember is looking in
on strangers eating in restaurants in Morrison or Clinton,
the glowing staple behind the name *forever*.

Black Tea and Trakl

Everything I know about aloneness
I learned from the large green rose I used
to trick my brain into having lucid dreams.
The procedure is relatively simple:
basically you picture any picture clearly
and let it stand for your desire to remain
in control after losing consciousness.
The transition should be gradual, as gradual
as looking away from the huge steel warehouse
that blocks the dorm's view of the river walk
without actually seeing the statue of Spiderman's
hands a handful of lunatics believe are the devil's,
nor noticing the salad fork made of absolute
smoothness wedged between the wall unit
and the pair of leaky pipes. Another piece
of advice would be to apply early, then think
of something recent that made you feel
a strong feeling. This evening when I attempt
the method as a demonstration for myself,
however, in the area where I normally experience
emotion, there's barely any activity to speak of.
Just a stunted auburn spark here and there,
and the miniscule shimmery puff I imagine is
the realization that I drank too much oolong
today. It was certainly warm out, and bright.
Some lanes were shadily narrow, perfect for eluding
the officers. As soon as it seemed I'd solved the puzzle
of the week, four of five missing letters changed
places and I couldn't recall whether the busted microscope
parts I accidentally glued to the desk in my dream dorm
ever made it home—but of this, at least, I was certain:
much that remains unknown between the real
and the other-than-real will be revealed, like a cobweb
building itself into the wallpaper of a house where no one
lives, or when a rousing speech can be translated
into a visual medium, which preserves an enthusiasm
for learning. As if a resonance has taken over.

The Case of the Arm

For a week my left arm tingled.
On several occasions
when I stood on my desk at the institute
overcome with waves of light-headedness
mixed with nostalgia for autumn walks
before the flood of '93, I saw blue and red planes.

Between one and four
I wandered the footpaths behind the institute
and tried to conjure up Mike from Long Beach's
last name, while the Blue Angels cut waves
in half up Evans Shore.
Usually somewhere a branch moves
and I discover something ultra-minute
like a zip-lock bag full of baby carrots
or the thought that perception
is fundamentally inductive.

I think that's why I still come out here
to see the one catfish emerge before the fireflies.
Questions spawning in the spaces between scales
pulsate in time with this pain in my arm
just long enough to make it hum a little
like a grace note over a chord.

Portrait of Tranströmer as a Fisherman

Bleached fish bones stretched on a stone slab.
Mute fortresses lighting the Black
Sea. Torches. When the sea turns.
In the same
turn what falls prey to the sea
where it thickens. Unseeable.
To disregard the non-mirror
parts. The bone bits. To heal. I mean
to be healed, it wants to be healed.
The sea does.
And the stone in the low voice
which mirrored this passage like the next
day disappears. It is a strategy. It is a joke
strategy, disappearing behind
the thought of it.
The thought of beaten seawater.
Apartness. Blackened bones
in the place beneath the word for impending storm
in underwater language.

Dangerous Museum

The museum was dangerous.
I smelled smoke and my mind changed.

There was a field recording
of an arctic moth's shadow

translated into a smoke ring.
It tasted like clean water

and was. A whole cup.
I almost felt like praying,

and I haven't prayed in centuries.
Then the weather melted.

Music came and went.
I opened a cabinet, an insect

we couldn't identify flew out.
We loved less and more than possible.

Acknowledgements

A special thanks to Henry Stanton and everyone at UnCollected Press for making this dream a reality, as well as the editors of the following journals, in which these poems first appeared:

"Paperclips of Various Sizes," "Walking Home from the Hospital," and "The Vampire" have appeared in *Forklift, OH*.

"National Geographic" has appeared in *Narrative Magazine*.

"Portrait of Transtromer as a Fisherman" has appeared in *Bridge*.

"Carrying Half-Rotten Fruit Over the Platforms of the Floating World" has appeared in *BARNHOUSE*.

"This Poem Is No Longer In Use," "The Franssen Effect," and "Dangerous Museum" have appeared in *Deluge*.

"I Woke Up in a Field," "The Language of Flowers Is in Much Disrepair," and "The Case of the Arm" have appeared in *The Raw Art Review*.

Biography

Adam Edelman grew up among the cornfields of central Iowa. He holds a BA in religious studies from the University of Iowa, and an MFA in poetry from the New Writers Project at the University of Texas at Austin, where he received a fellowship from the Michener Center for Writers. He currently lives in Austin, Texas with his wife Amrita, and is a PhD candidate in the Program for Writers at the University of Illinois at Chicago.

www.ingramcontent.com/pod-product-compliance
Lightning Source LLC
Chambersburg PA
CBHW021002090426
42736CB00010B/1426